Slim Goodbody's
BODY BUDDIES
Present...

THE DYNAMIC DIGESTIVE SYSTEM

How does my stomach work?

CRABTREE
Publishing Company
www.crabtreebooks.com

Crabtree Publishing Company
www.crabtreebooks.com

Series Development, Writing, and Packaging:
   John Burstein Slim Goodbody Corp.

Medical Reviewer:
   Christine S. Burstein, RN, MSN, FNP

Designer: Tammy West, Westgraphix

Project coordinator: Robert Walker

Editors: Mark Sachner, Water Buffalo Books
   Reagan Miller

Proofreader: Crystal Sikkens

Production coordinator: Katherine Berti

Prepress technicians: Rosie Gowsell,
   Katherine Berti, Ken Wright

Picture credits:
© istockphoto: p. 20b, 20c, 21a, 21b,
   21c, 21d, 25a, 27c
© Shutterstock: p. 7a, 7b, 7c, 7d, 13,
   25b, 26a
© Slim Goodbody: cover, p. 6, 9, 11, 13b, 15a,
   13b, 13c, 13d, 13e, 20a, 21e, 23, 24, 25c, 26b

Gurgle Character Design and Illustration:
   Mike Ray, Ink Tycoon

Medical Illustrations: Colette Sands,
   Render Ranch, and Mike Ray

"Slim Goodbody," "Gurgle," and Render Ranch
illustrations, copyright © Slim Goodbody

Library and Archives Canada Cataloguing in Publication

Burstein, John
    The dynamic digestive system : how does my stomach
work? / John Burstein.

(Slim Goodbody's body buddies)
Includes index.
ISBN 978-0-7787-4415-3 (bound).--ISBN 978-0-7787-4429-0 (pbk.)

    1. Gastrointestinal system--Juvenile literature. 2. Digestion--Juvenile
literature. I. Title. II. Series: Burstein, John . Slim Goodbody's body
buddies.

QP145.B87 2009   j612.3   C2008-907850-0

Library of Congress Cataloging-in-Publication Data

Burstein, John.
  The dynamic digestive system : how does my stomach work? /
John Burstein.
    p. cm. -- (Slim Goodbody's body buddies)
  Includes index.
  ISBN 978-0-7787-4429-0 (pbk. : alk. paper) -- ISBN 978-0-7787-4415-3
(reinforced library binding : alk. paper)
    1. Gastrointestinal system--Juvenile literature. 2. Digestion--Juvenile
literature. 3. Stomach--Juvenile literature. I. Title. II. Series.

  QP145.B87 2009
  612.3'2--dc22

                                          2008052373

Crabtree Publishing Company
www.crabtreebooks.com   1-800-387-7650

Published in Canada
Crabtree Publishing
616 Welland Ave.
St. Catharines, Ontario
L2M 5V6

Published in the United States
Crabtree Publishing
PMB16A
350 Fifth Ave., Suite 3308
New York, NY 10118

Published in the United Kingdom
Crabtree Publishing
White Cross Mills
High Town, Lancaster
LA1 4XS

Published in Australia
Crabtree Publishing
386 Mt. Alexander Rd.
Ascot Vale (Melbourne)
VIC 3032

About the Author
John Burstein (also known as Slim Goodbody) has been entertaining and educating children
for over thirty years. His programs have been broadcast on CBS, PBS, Nickelodeon, USA,
and Discovery. He has won numerous awards including the Parent's Choice Award and the
President's Council's Fitness Leader Award. Currently, Mr. Burstein tours the country with his
multimedia live show "Bodyology." For more information, please visit **slimgoodbody.com**.

CONTENTS

MEET THE BODY BUDDIES 4

GREETINGS 6

TERRIFIC TEETH 8

FOOD TUBE 10

MY TURN! 12

TWISTS AND TURNS 14

THE END OF THE LINE 16

THE DIGESTIVE SYSTEM 18

GOOD NUTRIENTS, GOOD NUTRITION 20

PYRAMID POWER 22

CRUMMY TUMMY 24

STOMACH SECRETS 26

FABULOUS PHRASES 28

AMAZING FACTS ABOUT YOUR DIGESTIVE SYSTEM . . . 29

GLOSSARY 30

FOR MORE INFORMATION 31

INDEX 32

Words in **bold** are defined in the glossary on page 30.

Meet the Body Buddies

HELLO. MY NAME IS SLIM GOODBODY.

I am very happy that you are reading this book. It means that you want to learn about your body!

I believe that the more you know about how your body works, the prouder you will feel.

I believe that the prouder you feel, the more you will do to take care of yourself.

I believe that the more you do to take care of yourself, the happier and healthier you will be.

To provide you with the very best information about how your body works, I have put together a team of good friends. I call them my Body Buddies, and I hope they will become your Body Buddies, too!

Let me introduce them to you:

- HUFF AND PUFF will guide you through the lungs and the respiratory system.

- TICKER will lead you on a journey to explore the heart and circulatory system.

- COGNOS will explain how the brain and nervous system work.

- SQUIRT will let you in on the secrets of tiny glands that do big jobs.

- FLEX AND STRUT will walk you through the workings of your bones and muscles.

- GURGLE will give you a tour of the stomach and digestive system.

HUFF & PUFF Say...
YOUR RESPIRATORY SYSTEM IS MADE UP OF YOUR LUNGS, ALL THE AIRWAYS CONNECTED WITH THEM, AND THE MUSCLES THAT HELP YOU BREATHE.

TICKER Says...
YOUR CIRCULATORY SYSTEM IS MADE UP OF YOUR HEART, WHICH PUMPS YOUR BLOOD, AND THE TUBES, CALLED BLOOD VESSELS, THROUGH WHICH YOUR BLOOD FLOWS.

COGNOS Says...
YOUR NERVOUS SYSTEM IS MADE UP OF YOUR BRAIN, **SPINAL CORD**, AND ALL THE NERVES THAT RUN THROUGHOUT YOUR BODY.

SQUIRT Says...
YOUR ENDOCRINE SYSTEM IS MADE UP OF MANY DIFFERENT GLANDS THAT PRODUCE SUBSTANCES TO HELP YOUR BODY WORK AS IT SHOULD.

GURGLE Says...
YOUR DIGESTIVE SYSTEM HELPS TURN THE FOOD YOU EAT INTO ENERGY. IT INCLUDES YOUR STOMACH, LIVER, AND INTESTINES.

FLEX & STRUT Say...
YOUR MUSCULAR SYSTEM IS MADE UP OF MUSCLES THAT HELP YOUR BODY MOVE. THE SKELETAL SYSTEM IS MADE UP OF THE BONES THAT SUPPORT YOUR BODY.

GREETINGS

HELLO.

MY NAME IS GURGLE, AND I AM A STOMACH. I AM PART OF A WONDERFUL TEAM CALLED THE DIGESTIVE SYSTEM. THIS BOOK WILL EXPLAIN WHAT MY TEAM MEMBERS AND I DO. IF YOU ARE HUNGRY FOR KNOWLEDGE, READ ON!

BREAKING IT DOWN

Your body is made up of trillions of **cells**. These cells are so tiny you could not see them without a powerful microscope. Cells need energy from food, but the food you eat is too big to fit inside these cells. It must be broken down into tiny bits that are smaller than cells. These tiny bits are called **nutrients**. The digestive system works to break down food into nutrients.

COGNOS says... NUTRIENTS ARE SOURCES OF NOURISHMENT AND ENERGY THAT COME FROM THE FOOD WE EAT.

THE LONG CANAL

Your digestive system is made up of your esophagus, stomach, small intestine, and large intestine. All of these digestive organs are connected. Together, they form a tube called the **alimentary canal**. The alimentary canal extends from the back of your throat all the way down to the end of your large intestine. Other organs, such as the liver, pancreas, and kidneys, help your digestive system.

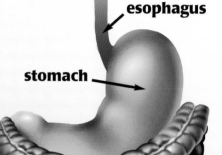

esophagus

stomach

small intestine

large intestine

pancreas

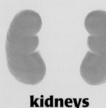

kidneys

liver

BE A SCIENTIST

This activity will help you understand why your digestive system must break food down into tiny nutrients.

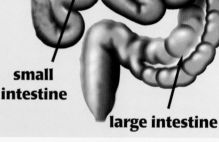

Here is what you will need:
- A piece of paper
- A pencil
- A raisin

Directions:

1. Use the pencil to make a small dot on the piece of paper.

2. Put the raisin down next to the dot.

3. Think about how you could fit the raisin into the dot.

The dot may be small, but it is many times bigger than a cell! Your digestive system works hard to break food down into pieces even smaller than cells.

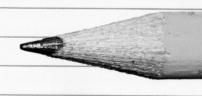

TERRIFIC TEETH

> DIGESTION DOES NOT START DOWN HERE WITH ME. IT BEGINS UP ABOVE—IN YOUR MOUTH. YOUR TERRIFIC TEETH BEGIN THE PROCESS OF DIGESTION BY CUTTING, TEARING, CRUSHING, AND GRINDING UP THE FOOD YOU EAT. THE **SALIVA** IN YOUR MOUTH HELPS DIGESTION AS WELL.

GET WET

Saliva is the clear liquid in your mouth. Saliva is mostly made of water. Saliva contains a few chemicals as well. Without saliva, food, such as a piece of toast, would be dry, scratchy, and difficult to get down. Saliva makes it much easier to swallow. As you chew, saliva wets the food and softens it. The chemicals in the saliva start to **dissolve** the food. Saliva is produced by salivary glands located inside your mouth.

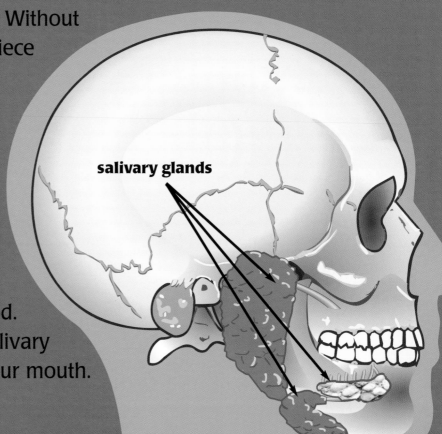

salivary glands

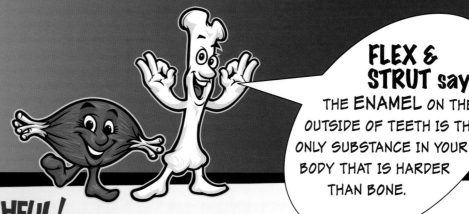

FLEX & STRUT say...
THE ENAMEL ON THE OUTSIDE OF TEETH IS THE ONLY SUBSTANCE IN YOUR BODY THAT IS HARDER THAN BONE.

WHAT A MOUTHFUL!

As soon as you put food in your mouth, your teeth get to work. Different teeth do different jobs:

1. Incisors are the sharp teeth in the front of your mouth. They cut food like a pair of scissors cuts paper.

2. Cuspids are right next to the incisors. Cuspids tear food into smaller bits. Cuspids get their name because each tooth has a point, or cusp, on top. Cuspids are also called canines.

3. Bicuspids are next to the cuspids. Bicuspids have two cusps on each tooth. Bicuspids crush food.

4. Molars are in the back of your mouth. Molars have four or five cusps on them. Molars grind food into tiny bits.

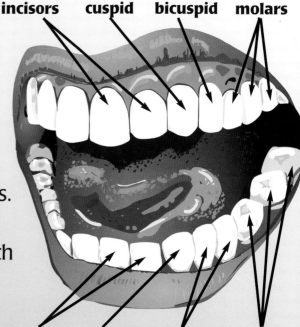

incisors   cuspid   bicuspid   molars

incisors   cuspid   bicuspids   molars

TONGUE FUN

Your tongue works hard to help digestion. As your teeth chew, your tongue pushes the food around and forms it into soft round balls. These balls get pushed to the back of your throat for you to swallow down. A single ball of food is called a **bolus**.

FOOD TUBE

WHEN YOU SWALLOW YOUR FOOD, IT MOVES THROUGH A FOOD TUBE CALLED THE ESOPHAGUS. THE ESOPHAGUS STARTS AT THE BACK OF YOUR THROAT AND LEADS RIGHT TO ME.

DOWN WE GO

Food does not drop through your esophagus like a barrel going over Niagara Falls. Food is pushed along by the muscles that line your esophagus. These muscles are involuntary muscles. Involuntary muscles work without you thinking about them. Your esophagus is a tube that is 8–10 inches (20–25 cm) long. The trip from the back of your mouth to your stomach takes 2–4 seconds. Liquids are also pushed along by muscles, although liquids reach the stomach more quickly than food.

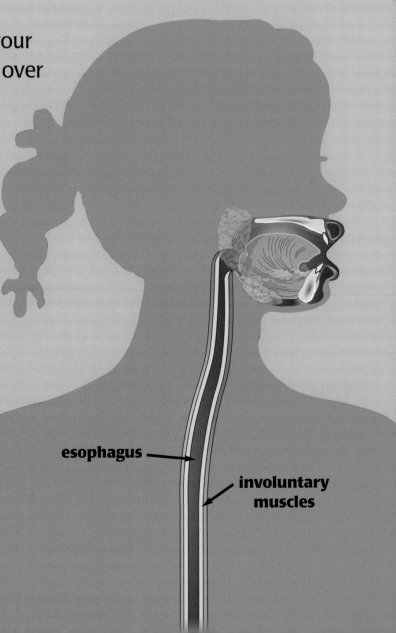

esophagus

involuntary muscles

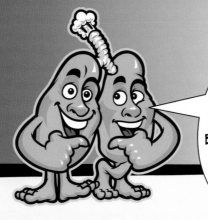

HUFF & PUFF say...
YOUR ESOPHAGUS RUNS DOWN YOUR NECK RIGHT BEHIND YOUR **TRACHEA**. YOUR TRACHEA IS YOUR WINDPIPE.

RIPPLING ALONG

The muscles in your esophagus use a rippling motion to move the food along. This rippling motion is called **peristalsis**. Here is how it works:

1. First, the upper muscles in the esophagus squeeze. This action forces the food down toward the stomach.

2. The next group of muscles in line squeezes to force the food down further.

3. Then the next group of muscles in line squeezes and forces the food down even more.

4. This motion goes on until the food reaches your stomach.

esophagus

food

muscles

to stomach

BE A SCIENTIST

You can prove that food is pushed along by the powerful muscles of your esophagus.

Directions:

1. Ask your parent to help you stand on your head.

2. Collect some saliva in your mouth.

3. Swallow the saliva.

If the muscles in your esophagus did not push the saliva to your stomach, it would just drop back into your mouth.

Here is what you will need:
- A pillow
- A parent

11

My Turn!

WHEN THE FOOD FINALLY REACHES ME, I GO TO WORK. I TWIST. I MIX. I CHURN. IT CAN TAKE ME TWO TO FIVE HOURS TO FINISH MY JOB.

J SHAPE

Your stomach is a stretchy bag of muscles shaped like the letter "J." Your stomach has three important jobs:

1. It holds the food you have eaten.

2. It breaks down the food into **chyme**.

3. It empties the chyme into your small intestine.

stomach

GURGLE says...
MUCUS IS A SLIPPERY SUBSTANCE THAT COATS AND PROTECTS THE STOMACH WALLS. BECAUSE THE WALLS OF YOUR STOMACH ARE LINED WITH MUCUS, THEY ARE NOT HURT BY STRONG GASTRIC JUICES.

ACID IN ACTION

Your stomach is lined with muscles. These muscles mix and mash the food you swallow. As the stomach works, it releases **gastric** acid. This acid contains strong chemicals that break down food. Gastric acid also helps kill any germs that might have been in the food when you ate it. By the time your stomach has completed its work, food has been changed into a thick liquid called chyme.

gastric acid   **stomach**

BE A SCIENTIST

This experiment will help demonstrate why food that is broken down dissolves into a liquid more easily.

Here is what you will need:
- Two glasses of water
- A sugar cube
- A spoonful of sugar
- Two spoons

Directions:

1. Drop the sugar cube in one glass of water.

2. Pour the spoonful of sugar into the other glass of water.

3. Use the two spoons to stir both glasses at the same time.

The sugar that is already broken down into small particles should dissolve more quickly.

13

THE END OF THE LINE

SOME PARTS OF FOOD CANNOT BE BROKEN DOWN INTO NUTRIENTS. THESE PARTS INCLUDE FRUIT SKINS, THE OUTER LAYERS OF GRAINS, AND STRINGY PIECES OF VEGETABLES. THESE LEFTOVERS MOVE INTO THE LARGE INTESTINE. THE JOURNEY OF FOOD IS COMING TO AN END.

LONG AND SHORT

Your large intestine is much shorter than your small intestine. It is only about 4–5 feet (1–1.5 m) long. If you stretched your large intestine out, it would only be about as tall as you are. The large intestine is called "large" because of its width. It is more than twice as wide as the small intestine.

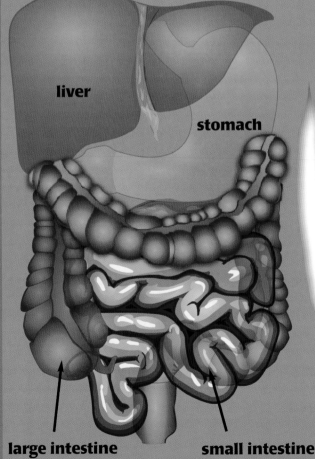

liver

stomach

large intestine

small intestine

WHAT HAPPENS TO WASTE

Here is what happens as waste builds up in the large intestine:

1. The muscles that line the walls of the large intestine start squeezing.

2. Waste gets pushed toward the end of the large intestine.

3. The waste passes into the colon, or lower part of the large intestine.

4. In the colon, any remaining liquid or nutrients are removed.

5. The waste gets harder and harder, until it becomes a solid.

6. The solid waste is pushed into the last section of the large intestine called the rectum.

7. When you go to the bathroom, the waste is pushed out of the opening at the end of the rectum. This opening is called the anus.

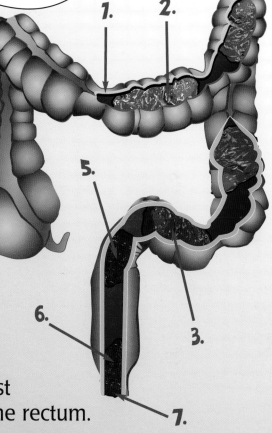

LIQUID WASTE

You have two kidneys located in the middle of your back on either side of your spine. Kidneys filter out waste in the blood. This waste is combined with water to make **urine**.

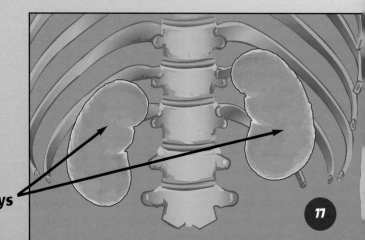

kidneys

THE DIGESTIVE SYSTEM

salivary glands

esophagus

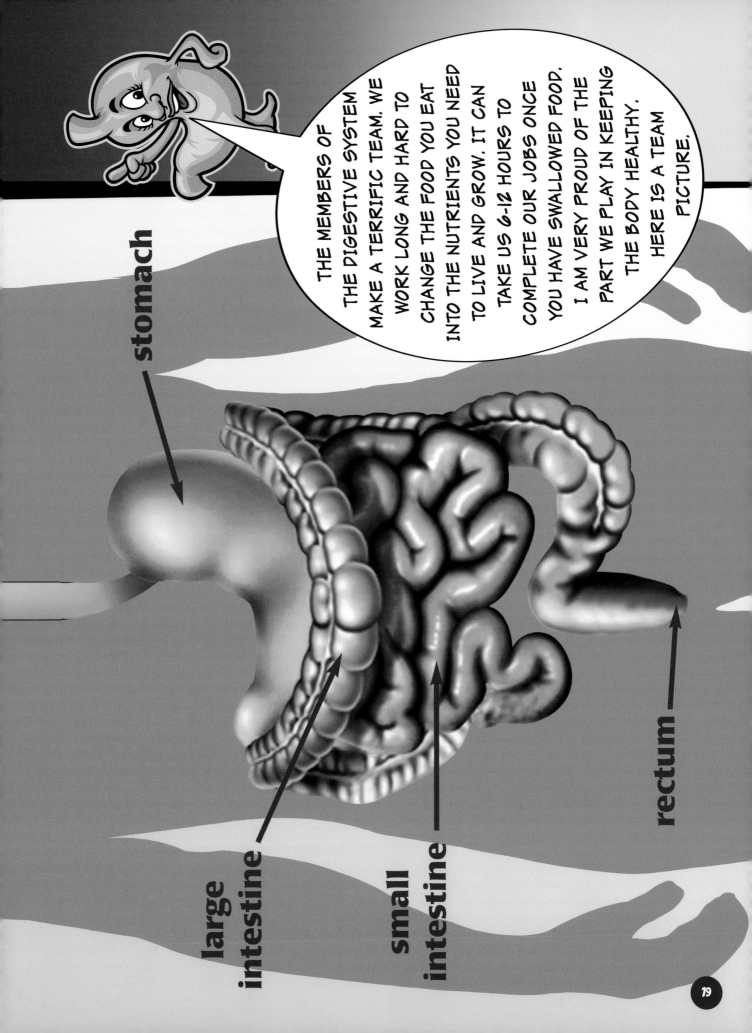

Good Nutrients, Good Nutrition

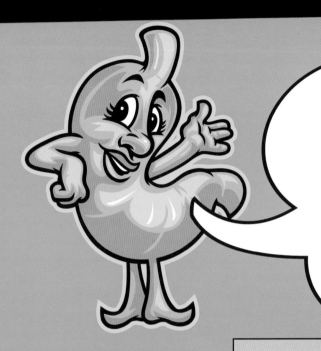

I KNOW A LOT ABOUT FOOD AND WHAT THE BODY NEEDS. I KNOW THAT NO SINGLE FOOD CONTAINS ALL THE NUTRIENTS YOU NEED. TO STAY HEALTHY, PEOPLE MUST GET A VARIETY OF NUTRIENTS EVERY DAY.

STICK WITH SIX

Your digestive system breaks food down into six different nutrients. Each nutrient does something different for your body.

1. Carbohydrates give you energy to run, jump, play, and think. You get carbohydrates from fruits, vegetables, cereals, breads, and pasta.

2. Proteins are used to build and repair cells. You get proteins from meat, fish, beans, milk, yogurt, cheeses, and eggs.

3. Fats help make you feel full and provide a soft, protective cushion around your organs. You get fats from butter, cheeses, salad dressings, olive oil, and nuts.

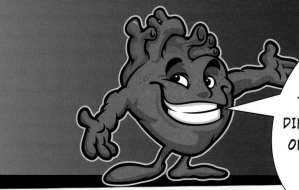

TICKER says... EVERY ORGAN IN THE BODY USES A DIFFERENT COMBINATION OF NUTRIENTS TO GET ITS JOB DONE.

5. Vitamins help keep your eyes healthy. Vitamins also help protect against **infection**. You get many vitamins from fruits and vegetables.

6. Water helps make up your blood, sweat, saliva, urine, and mucus. There is some water in all the foods you eat.

4. Minerals help build strong bones and strong teeth. You get minerals from fruits, vegetables, meats, nuts, grains, and dairy products.

BE A SCIENTIST

Here is one way you can find out if a food contains fats.

Directions:

1. Put the butter and the slice of apple on the paper towel.

2. Wait one minute.

3. Remove the butter and apple from the paper towel.

If the food has fat in it, it will leave an oily, greasy spot on the paper towel. If the spot is wet, but not oily and greasy, then the food does not have fat. Which food contains fat?

Here is what you will need:
- A paper towel
- A little butter
- A slice of apple
- A clock

27

Pyramid Power

CHOOSING THE RIGHT FOODS MIGHT SEEM CONFUSING AT FIRST. YOU CANNOT GO TO A RESTAURANT AND ORDER A PLATE OF CARBOHYDRATES WITH SOME MINERALS ON THE SIDE! TO HELP YOU FIGURE OUT HOW TO GET THE PROPER NUTRIENTS, I SUGGEST YOU USE THE FOOD PYRAMID.

SPECIAL STRIPES

Use the Food Pyramid to help you choose a healthy diet. The food pyramid has six different stripes. Each stripe stands for a different food group. Some stripes are wider than others. The wider the stripe, the more food you need from that group every day.

Each stripe is also wider at the base and gets thinner at the top. Eat more foods that are at the base of each stripe. These foods are usually in their "natural" form. That means you do not have to prepare them too much before eating.

MyPyramid.gov
STEPS TO A HEALTHIER YOU

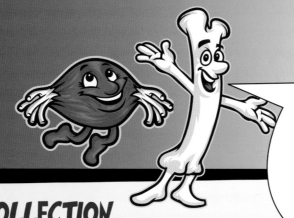

FLEX & STRUT say... LOOK AT THE FOOD PYRAMID. THERE IS A PERSON CLIMBING UP THE STEPS. THIS PICTURE REMINDS US THAT EXERCISE IS ALSO IMPORTANT FOR GOOD HEALTH.

A COLORFUL COLLECTION

ORANGE The orange stripe stands for grains, like breads, cereals, rice, and pasta. At the base of the stripe are healthy whole grains like whole wheat bread and oatmeal. At the top are cakes, cupcakes, donuts, and sugary foods.

RED The red stripe stands for fruits. Fresh fruits like apples, pears, and oranges belong at the base. Sugary fruit juices and apple pie belong at the top.

PURPLE The purple stripe stands for meat, chicken, fish, seeds, and nuts. Broiled chicken belongs at the base. Fatty meats and fried chicken belong on top.

GREEN The green stripe stands for vegetables. Fresh vegetables like carrots, cucumbers, and broccoli belong at the base. French fries belong on top because they are not very healthy.

BLUE The blue stripe stands for dairy products. Low-fat milk, yogurt, and cheeses belong at the base. Ice cream and butter belong at the top.

YELLOW The yellow stripe is the thinnest of all. It stands for oils like corn and canola oil. You only need a little oil everyday.

CRUMMY TUMMY

SOMETIMES I GET SICK. WHEN I FEEL BAD, I DO NOT DO MY JOB AS WELL AS USUAL. I MIGHT CHURN THE FOOD TOO FAST. I MIGHT CHURN THE FOOD TOO SLOW. I MIGHT MIX IN TOO MUCH GASTRIC JUICE, OR NOT ENOUGH. WHEN I AM HAVING TROUBLE, I NEED YOU TO TAKE EXTRA SPECIAL CARE OF ME!

I FEEL UPSET

Digestive problems can make us feel sick. They can also be a little embarrassing, but everyone gets them at one time or another. Here are some of the most common problems:

INDIGESTION Indigestion is another name for an upset stomach. You might get indigestion if you eat too quickly, eat too much, or eat foods that are too spicy. If you have indigestion, you will probably feel pain in your abdomen. You might feel bloated, as if you ate too much—or nauseous, as if you want to throw up.

GURGLE says... NOBODY KNOWS FOR CERTAIN WHY PEOPLE HAVE FOOD **ALLERGIES.** FOR SOME REASON, WHAT IS HARMLESS TO MOST PEOPLE, LIKE MILK OR PEANUT BUTTER, CAN CAUSE PROBLEMS FOR OTHERS.

TOO LITTLE—CONSTIPATION

Constipation means waste builds up in your large intestine and you are not having bowel movements as often as you should. If you have fewer than three bowel movements a week and your **stool** is dry and hard to pass, you may be constipated. Drinking a lot of fluids and eating **fiber** can help.

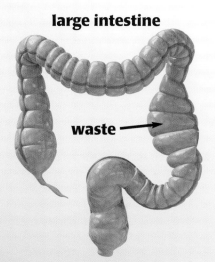

large intestine

waste →

TOO MUCH—DIARRHEA

When you have diarrhea, you go to the bathroom much more often than usual. Your bowel movements are loose and watery. Diarrhea is often caused by germs. It can also be caused by eating spicy or greasy foods.

UP AND OUT—VOMITING

Vomiting happens when the muscles in your stomach, intestines, or abdomen push food up instead of down. Food is pushed back up to your mouth. It comes out mashed up and watery, with saliva and gastric juices mixed in.

25

Stomach Secrets

A LONG TIME AGO, PEOPLE DID NOT KNOW WHAT HAPPENED TO FOOD AFTER IT WAS SWALLOWED. DIGESTION WAS A BIG MYSTERY. NOBODY KNEW HOW I WORKED. IT TOOK MANY YEARS AND MANY SMART SCIENTISTS TO UNLOCK MY SECRETS!

SOLVING THE MYSTERY

Scientists have been studying the digestive system for many years. Some of their most important work was begun over 250 years ago!

GASTRIC DISCOVERY

René de Réaumur, a French scientist living in 1750, wanted to find out how the stomach worked. He experimented with his pet bird. He took a tiny metal tube, put sponges in it, and slipped it into the food the bird ate. The bird swallowed the tube and, soon after, vomited it out. René took the sponges out of the tube and found they weighed five times more than when he had put them in. When he squeezed out the sponges, he discovered the sponges contained juice. He called the juice *gastric juice*.

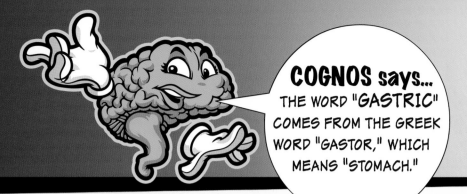

COGNOS says... THE WORD "GASTRIC" COMES FROM THE GREEK WORD "GASTOR," WHICH MEANS "STOMACH."

IN THE BAG

Lazaro Spallanzani was an Italian scientist living in 1780 who experimented on himself! He chewed a little food, placed it in a tiny linen bag with a string attached, and swallowed it. Later, when he pulled the bag up, it was empty. He realized that the gastric juices in his stomach had dissolved the chewed food.

Lazaro Spallanzani

HOLE IN ONE

Dr. Beaumont

Dr. William Beaumont was a U.S. Army doctor. In 1822, he cared for a wounded soldier named Alexis St. Martin. Alexis had been shot, and the bullet had made a large hole in his stomach. Alexis got better, but the hole never completely closed. There was just a flap of skin covering it. Dr. Beaumont could lift the flap and watch the stomach working! Over the next 10 years, Dr. Beaumont did over 100 experiments. He learned that the stomach finished work on some foods faster than on others. Foods like bread and potatoes were ready to leave the stomach in about an hour. Foods like meat and eggs stayed in the stomach for three or four hours longer.

FABULOUS PHRASES

BEFORE I LEAVE YOU, I WANT TO PLAY A LITTLE GAME. IN THE BOX BELOW YOU WILL SEE EIGHT PHRASES. EACH PHRASE HAS THE WORD "STOMACH" IN IT. I WILL START A SENTENCE AND YOU TRY TO FILL IN THE BLANK USING ONE OF THE PHRASES.

FOR EXAMPLE, IF SENTENCE NUMBER 1 IS: SOMEONE WHO FEELS NAUSEOUS JUST LOOKING AT FOOD HAS A_____

YOU WOULD CHOOSE THE PHRASE "F": "WEAK STOMACH." GOT IT?

Remember, choose a phrase that completes the sentence. The right matches are at the bottom of the page.
But you will have to turn the book upside down to read them!

1. Someone who feels nauseous just looking at food has a _____.

2. If you order too much food in a restaurant but cannot eat it, someone might say that your eyes are _____.

3. People who can eat all kinds of spicy foods without getting sick have a _____.

4. If you refuse to do something because you know it is wrong, you just_____.

5. When you feel nervous about something, someone might say you have _____.

6. If someone shows you something really disgusting, you might say that it _____.

A. cast-iron stomach	**C.** bigger than your stomach	**E.** turns my stomach
B. cannot stomach it	**D.** butterflies in your stomach	**F.** weak stomach

Amazing Facts About Your Digestive System

EMOTIONS AFFECT DIGESTION! WHEN YOU ARE WORRIED OR UNHAPPY, YOUR STOMACH AND INTESTINES DO NOT WORK AS WELL AS WHEN YOU ARE HAPPY OR CAREFREE.

THE STOMACH CAN CHANGE ITS SHAPE DEPENDING ON THE AMOUNT OF FOOD IN IT.

HEARTBURN HAS NOTHING TO DO WITH YOUR HEART. IT IS A BURNING SENSATION IN THE AREA OF YOUR HEART, BUT IT IS CAUSED BY ACID FROM YOUR STOMACH THAT BACKS UP INTO THE ESOPHAGUS.

THE STOMACH'S DIGESTIVE ACIDS ARE STRONG ENOUGH TO DISSOLVE SOME METALS.

YOUR LIVER IS THE LARGEST SOLID ORGAN IN YOUR BODY. BY THE TIME YOU ARE FULLY GROWN, YOUR LIVER WILL BE ABOUT THE SIZE OF A FOOTBALL.

YOU PRODUCE ABOUT 1 QUART (1 L) OF SALIVA EVERY DAY.

ABOUT 2 QUARTS (1.9 L) OF FOOD AND LIQUIDS PASS THROUGH YOUR BODY EACH DAY.

MOST MILK AND MILK PRODUCTS WE USE COME FROM COWS. MANY PEOPLE AROUND THE WORLD USE MILK THAT COMES FROM OTHER ANIMALS, SUCH AS GOATS, YAKS, SHEEP, AND BUFFALO.

YOUR BODY USES FOOD TO GROW. EACH YEAR, A CHILD GROWS AN AVERAGE OF 3 INCHES (8 CM) AND GAINS AN AVERAGE OF 5 POUNDS (2 KG).

GLOSSARY

abdomen The part of the body, often called the belly, that contains the digestive organs

alimentary canal The passage that extends from the back of your throat to the end of the large intestine

bolus A small ball of chewed food just as it is about to be swallowed

cells The smallest units, or structures, that make up the body. Cells are so tiny that they cannot be seen without a microscope

chyme A thick liquid formed in the stomach and passed on to the small intestine, consisting mostly of gastric juices and partly digested food

dissolve To mix a solid substance, such as sugar or salt, into a liquid so that the substance becomes part of the liquid or evenly spread throughout the liquid

gastric Having to do with the stomach

fiber A material found in food containing cellulose and other substances that digestive juices do not break down easily and that are not absorbed into the body's cells

infection The attack on healthy parts of the body by germs. Infections can lead to injury or disease and should be cleaned and treated with medicine

peristalsis The contracting and expanding motion of the muscles throughout the alimentary canal that moves food along from the esophagus through the stomach and the intestines

saliva A clear liquid produced by glands around the mouth

spinal cord A cord of nerve tissue running through the middle of the backbone

stool Solid waste matter as it is ready to leave the body through the rectum

urine Liquid containing excess water, salt, and other substances not needed by the body and removed from the blood by kidneys

villi Hair-like projections in the walls of the small intestine that help move along food as it is being digested

FOR MORE INFORMATION

BOOKS

Disgusting Digestion (Horrible Science). Nick Arnold. Scholastic.

Guts: Our Digestive System. Seymour Simon. HarperCollins.

Janice VanCleave's Food and Nutrition for Every Kid: Easy Activities That Make Learning Science Fun (Science for Every Kid Series). Janice VanCleave. Wiley.

The Quest to Digest. Mary K. Corcoran. Charlesbridge Publishing.

YUM: Your Ultimate Manual for Good Nutrition. Daina Kalnins. Lobster Press.

WEBSITES

Discovery Kids
yucky.discovery.com/flash/body/pg000126.html
This website has a lot of information and very cool "yucky" interactive games to play.

Kidhealth
kidshealth.org/kid/htbw/digestive_system.html
Check out this website for information on your stomach and digestive system.

Kid Info
kidinfo.com/Health/Human_Body.html
This website provides many links you can follow to learn about all the systems of the human body.

National Museum of Dentistry
mouthpower.org/mouthpower.cfm
This is a terrific site where you can play games to learn how to care for your teeth and receive a Certificate of Achievement.

Slim Goodbody
www.slimgoodbody.com
Discover loads of fun and free downloads for kids, teachers, and parents.

INDEX

Abdomen 14, 24, 25
acids, digestive
    see gastric acids
        and juices
alimentary canal 7
allergies to food 25
anus 17

Blood 5, 14, 15,
    17, 21
bolus 9
bones 4, 5, 9, 21
bowel 17, 25
brain 4, 5

Cells 6, 7, 20
chyme 12, 13
colon 17

Digestion and digestive
    system 4, 5, 6, 7, 8,
        14, 18–19, 20, 24,
        26, 29, 31

Energy 5, 6, 7, 20
esophagus 7, 10, 11,
    18, 29

Fiber 25

food pyramid 22–23
Gastric acids and juices
    13, 24, 25, 26, 27, 29
germs 13, 25
Heart 4, 5, 29
Indigestion 24
intestines 5, 25, 29
    large 7, 16, 17,
        19, 25
    small 7, 12, 14,
        15, 16, 19
Kidneys 7, 17
Liver 5, 7, 15, 16, 29
Mouth 8, 9, 10, 11, 25
muscles 4, 5, 10, 11,
    12, 13, 17, 25
Nutrients 6, 7, 14,
    15, 16, 17, 18, 20,
    21, 22
nutrition 20–21,
    22–23
Organs 7, 20 29
Pancreas 7

peristalsis 11
Rectum 17, 19
respiratory system
    4, 5
Saliva and salivary
    glands 8, 11, 18,
        21, 25, 29
stomach 4, 5, 6, 7, 10,
    11, 12, 13, 14, 15, 16,
    19, 24, 25, 26, 27,
    28, 29, 31
    illness 24–25
    protection of 13
stool 25
swallowing 8, 9, 10,
    11, 13, 19, 26, 27
Teeth 8–9, 21, 31
throat 7, 9, 10
tongue 9
trachea (windpipe) 11
Urine 17, 21
Villi 15
Waste 15, 17, 25
water 8, 13, 17, 21, 25

Printed in the U.S.A. - CG